Here Comes The Bride

A COLLECTION OF TRADITIONAL WEDDING MUSI
FOR ORGAN / VOICE / PIANO
COMPILED AND ARRANGED BY FRED BOCK

TABLE OF CONTENTS

Might we suggest that you also consider the materials in WHOM GOD HATH JOINED TOGETHER, a wedding collection of contemporary selections for voice and organ/piano. Published by Fred Bock Music Company. Distributed by Hal Leonard Corp. Cat.# 08738433.

Fred Bock Music Company

Trumpet Air
(Processional)

OTHER ORGANS
Sw.   Trumpet solo stop 8'
Gt. or Ch. Diapason 8', soft flute 4'
Pedal Full 16', 8'

DRAWBAR ORGANS
Sw. 02 7878 678
Gt.   00 6837 335
Pedal 46

Henry Purcell
Arranged by Fred Bock

Trumpet Voluntary
(Processional)

OTHER ORGANS

Sw. Trumpet solo stop 8'
Gt. or Ch. Diapason 8', soft flute 4'
Gt. Full organ, 4' coupler
Pedal Full 16', 8'

DRAWBAR ORGANS

Sw. 02 7878 678
Gt. 00 6837 336
Pedal 54

Jeremiah Clark
Arranged by Fred Bock

Bridal Chorus
(Processional)

OTHER ORGANS

Sw.	Trumpet 8', Reeds 8', 4'
Gt.	Full organ 8', 4', 2', mixtures
Pedal	Full 16', 8'

DRAWBAR ORGANS

Sw.	02 7888 668
Gt.	00 6848 457
Pedal	55

Richard Wagner
Arranged by Fred Bock

Sw. *pp*

ppp

reduce ped.　　　　reduce ped.

A Mystical Moment

(Carillon)
from Three Mystical Moments

All manuals and Pedal: Full

Gordon Young

With increasing intensity

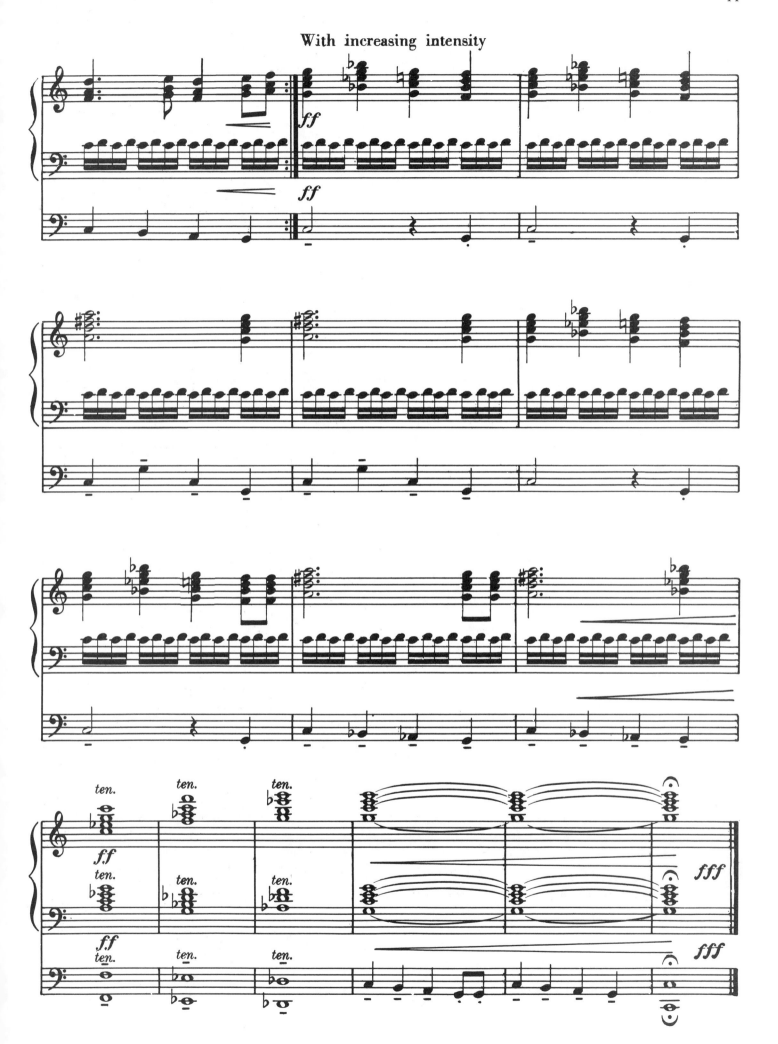

Pavane

from Rhythmic Suite

OTHER ORGANS

Sw.	Solo combination, strings predominating
Gt.	Flute 8'
Ch.	Flute 8', Gemshorn 8'
Pedal	Bourdon 16', Ch. to Ped.

DRAWBAR ORGANS

Sw.	00 8800 000
Gt.	00 5615 223
Pedal	43

Robert Elmore

Allegro in A
(Processional or Recessional)

OTHER ORGANS		DRAWBAR ORGANS	
Sw.	Flutes 8', 4'	Sw.	00 8008 004
Gt.	Full organ 8', 4', 4' coupler	Gt.	Preset G or 00 6636 035
Pedal	Full 16', 8'	Pedal	45

Fred Bock

Entreat Me Not to Leave Thee

Ruth 1:16,17

Gordon Young
Arranged by Fred Bock

As in the beginning

aught but death part thee and me._____ En-

treat me not to__ leave thee, or to re-turn from fol-low-ing af-ter thee: O en-

treat me not to leave thee, or to re-turn from fol-low-ing af-ter thee: for

whi-ther thou go-est, I will go;_____ and

where thou lod-gest, I will lodge: Thy peo-ple shall be my

peo-ple, and thy God, my God! En-treat me not to_ leave thee, O en-

treat me not to leave_ thee: En-treat me not, en-treat me not to

leave thee, to leave thee._

O Promise Me

Clement Scott

Reginald de Koven

poco rubato

a tempo

prom-ise me that you will take my hand, The most un-wor-thy in this lone-ly

land, And let me sit be-side you, in your eyes

See-ing the vi-sion of our par-a-dise, Hear-ing God's mes-sage while the

cresc.

largamente e con passione

colla voce

or - gan rolls Its might - y mu - sic to our

ver - y souls; No love less per-fect than a life with thee; O

prom-ise me! O prom - ise me!

con forza

rall. *ff*

a tempo *dim.*

rall.

p *pp*

Eternal Life

St. Francis of Assisi (1182-1226)

Olive Dungan
Arranged by Fred Bock

un-der-stood as to un-der - stand,_____ To be loved as to

love;_ For it is in giv-ing that we re - ceive;_ It

is in par-d'ning that we are par-doned; It is in

dy-ing that we are born_____ to e-ter - nal life._____

Panis Angelicus
(O Lord, Most Holy)

César Franck

sempre legato

O lov - ing Fa - ther, Thee would we be prais - ing
Dat pa - nis coe - li - cus fi - gu - ris ter - mi -

al - way. Help us to know_ Thee, know Thee and
num. O res mi - ra - bi - lis man - du - cat

sempre legato

love_ Thee; Fa - ther, Fa - ther, grant us Thy truth and
Do - mi - num, Pau - per, pau - per, ser - vus et hu - mi -

grace; Fa - ther, Fa - ther, guide and de - fend___

lis, *Pau - per,* *pau - per,* *(f) ser - vus et hu - mi -*

us.

lis.

Rule Thou our wil - ful hearts, Keep Thee our

Pa - nis an - ge - li - cus fit pa - nis

wan-d'ring thoughts; In all our sor - rows let us find our rest in
ho - mi - num (f) *Dat pa - nis coe - li - ous fi - gu - ris ter - mi -*

Thee; And in temp - ta - tion's hour, Save through Thy
num, O res mi - ra - bi - lis man - du - cat

might - y pow'r, Thine aid O send us; Hear
Do - mi - num, Pau - per, pau - per, ser -

Because

Edward Teschemacher

Guy d'Hardelot

Poco Adagio

Be - cause____ you come to me _____ with naught save love, ___ And hold my hand and lift mine eyes a - bove, __ A

Wedding Recessional
(A Majestic Medley)

OTHER ORGANS
Sw.   Full, no reeds
Gt.   Full, no reeds + 4' coupler
Pedal Full 16', 8'

DRAWBAR ORGANS
Sw.   Preset G#
Gt.   00 7837 457
Ped.   56

Felix Mendelssohn
Arranged by Fred Bock

42

*To extend this piece further, segue to *Praise God* on next page.

Praise God From Whom All Blessings Flow

Louis Bourgeouis
Arranged by Fred Bock

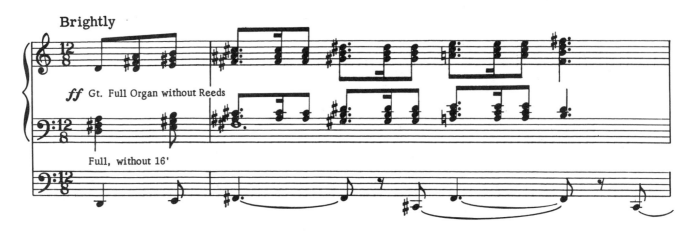

O Perfect Love

Dorothy Gurney

Joseph Barnby
Arranged by Fred Bock

1. O per - fect Love, all hu - man thought tran-scend - ing, Low - ly we kneel in pray'r be - fore Thy throne, That theirs may be the love which knows no end - ing, Whom Thou for-ev - er - more dost join in one.

2. O per - fect Life, be Thou their full as-sur - ance Of ten - der char - i - ty and stead - fast faith, Of pa - tient hope, and qui - et, brave en - dur - ance, With child - like trust that fears not pain nor death.

3. Grant them the joy which bright-ens earth - ly sor - row; Grant them the peace which calms all earth - ly strife, And to life's day the glo - rious un - known mor - row That dawns up-on e - ter - nal love and life.

Optional CODA